Coming to God

COMING TO GOD
IN THE STILLNESS

JIM BORST

eagle

Eagle Publishing, Bath

This edition, © 2007 Eagle Publishing Ltd, 3 & 4 The Drove, West Wilts Trading Estate, Westbury, Wiltshire, BA13 4JE.

Original edition published by Asian Trading Corporation, PO Box 11029, Mumbai, India, under the title *A Method of Contemplative Prayer.*

British Library Cataloguing in Publication Data. A catalogue record for this book is available from the British Library.

Typeset by Eagle Publishing Ltd
Printed by The Athenaeum Press.
ISBN No:978 0 86347 635 8

Contents

Foreword by Joyce Huggett 9
Part 1: The Twelve Stages of Prayer
1. A Method of Contemplative Prayer 19
Part 2: Some Questions Answered
2. What is Contemplation? 49
3. Why Practise Contemplative Prayer? 55
4. What Does Contemplation Achieve? 63
5. Where Should I Pray? 66
6. How Long Should I Pray? 67
7. When Should I Pray? 69
8. How Do I Deal with Distractions? 70
Epilogue 75
A Prayer 81
Notes 83
Bibliography 85

Foreword

In the mid-seventies, like many other Christians at that time, I found myself filled with a fresh longing for God. This prompted me to pray that God would touch me afresh with his Spirit. For nearly a year, in one way or another, I expressed this longing to God. I did not know then that Jim Borst's book existed. Even if I had been aware of it, I would not have dreamed that it would radically change my prayer life.

During that year, I was invited to speak about prayer at a student retreat which was being held at a monastery near my home. I had never visited this monastery before. I had never darkened the doors of any monastery or convent. So I did not expect, as I stood on the threshold of Mount St Bernard Abbey in Leicestershire, that within these walls God would begin to answer my hear-felt request in a significant and life-changing way.

That Saturday in November, I took my first sip of silence. It was the first of many. And that visit was the first of many. After this I went frequently to Mount St Bernard. Each time I discovered in that prayer-saturated place what it means to be so still before God that I could let go of my need to achieve and discover the awesome privilege of becoming aware of his presence and of receiving his love. I soaked up this love just as a sponge soaks up water. I opened myself to this love just as a water lily opens its petals to the warm rays of the sun. Each time I visited this house of prayer I would come away with a mixture of emotions. On one level I was deeply satisfied by the sense of the love of God. On another level, I felt parched and dry: always hungry for more – as though there existed within me a bottomless pit of desire which could easily be satisfied when I stilled myself in God's presence but which raged again when life became busy.

While I was praying with a friend one evening we became quite still. The sense of the presence and the power of the Risen Christ was strong. I suddenly became aware that my friend was echoing the prayer I had prayed secretly for so many months – that God would touch me afresh with his Holy Spirit; that he would fill the parched places of my life. The prayer, I knew, was being answered. Fresh energy and joy seemed to be surging into me. As I walked home later that evening, I tingled with this joy. It deprived me of sleep that night but I was glad to be awake, glad to have time to soak up more and more of the love of God which seemed to be sweeping over me and flooding my entire being.

The next few weeks were wonderful. Whether I was working in the house or walking to the shops, meeting the children from school or spending time with my husband, I was constantly aware that God's love was enveloping me in a way I had never experienced before although I had been a church-goer all my life and a committed Christian for over twenty years. This love so overwhelmed me that when I prayed I seemed to be stunned into silence. Suddenly there seemed to be no words to express what I wanted to say. Instead of simply sipping silence, being still before God became my normal way of praying. I did not attempt to understand what was happening, I simply accepted this change, recognising it as a gracious gift from a generous God in answer to the prayer which had been born of an acknowledged poverty of spirit.

A few months later, a friend lent me a book which set me on a journey. It claimed that when a person receives a fresh touch of God's Spirit through charismatic renewal, the laying on of hands or by any other means, one of the effects may well be that their prayer will change. One reason for this is that one of the tasks of the Holy Spirit is to teach us to pray. Another of his tasks is to *help* us to pray by praying through us. As Paul reminds us, when we are at a loss to know how to pray, 'the Spirit himself intercedes for us with groans that words cannot express', 'with sighs too deep for words', 'with inexpressible longings which God alone understands' (Rom. 8:26,27).

The author claimed that this inexpressible longing for God has a name: contemplative prayer.

As I read this book, the proverbial penny dropped. This still prayer I was enjoying and which seemed to come gift-wrapped from God not only had a name, it is a gift which often comes to people who open themselves to God's Spirit.

Since contemplative prayer seemed to be a well-tried method, I set myself the task of learning more about it. The problem was that I had no teacher.

But I had another friend who was as hungry for God as I was. When I visited her one Saturday afternoon, she handed me a small booklet saying: 'You might like to take a look at this'.

The booklet was printed on poor quality paper, the print

was smudged and the pages were held together by a plain, unattractive, buff dust jacket which bore no picture, only the title: *A Method of Contemplative Prayer.*

That title drew me as a bee to honeysuckle. And it underlined the fact that some books have a ministry out of all proportion to their size and appearance.

The author, Jim Borst, is a Dutch missionary who has worked in India since 1963. I warmed to him when I read that his timetable, like mine, is so full that prayer only happens when he uses his creativity to carve out space for it. I felt further drawn to him when I discovered that, despite the busyness, he does find time to pray and that prayer brings him such joy and relief that he longs to share his insights with others.

I realised that we have much in common: he stresses that prayer must have a firm foundation; that such foundations are laid when a person accepts Jesus as Lord and Saviour and becomes open to the Holy Spirit's infilling. The author's claim that a fresh touch of God's Spirit opens the door to contemplative prayer seemed to be addressed to me personally. I read the booklet avidly and found to my astonishment and delight, that James Borst was applying himself to the questions I was asking: What is contemplation? What does this kind of prayer achieve? How does one learn the art of contemplative prayer?

My friend, seeing my delight, warned that that evening she would have to return the booklet to the person who had lent it to her. And we could not buy our own copies because it had gone out of print.

There and then, I sat at her dining room table and copied out whole pages in long hand. Instinctively, I knew that I could not afford to allow such spiritual gems to slip through my fingers. My time was not wasted. As I wrote, my understanding of the nature of contemplative prayer increased and I longed to try out Jim Borst's step by step method of prayer.

Over the next few months my hand-written copy of this booklet became my constant companion. Then, to my joy, I discovered that the booklet had been re-printed so I abandoned the hand-written version in favour of the printed one.

Since this early discovery, I have read countless books on prayer but I come back time and again to that sixty-page, buff-coloured book whose pages are now well-worn and yellow with age. This booklet is so important to me that when readers write to express appreciation of my own books and to confess that their pilgrimage finds so many parallels with mine, I frequently find myself longing to be able to place in their hands Jim Borst's distilled wisdom.

When the Managing Director of Eagle, David Wavre, conceived the idea of publishing a series of books designed to help such people explore the pathway of prayer, I suggested we should launch the series with this simple but profound small book which bears the hallmarks of having been inspired by the Holy Spirit.

At first all efforts to trace the author proved abortive. We were on the verge of abandoning the attempt when we located him in Holland – about to return to India. With great generosity and trust, he gave us permission to reproduce this adaptation of his original manuscript and to illustrate it in way which would enhance the text and make it even more memorable for the reader. Having proved for myself over the past sixteen years the value of his twelve steps of contemplation, I have no hesitation in recommending *Coming To God* to all those who experience within themselves a desire to enter more deeply into a living, loving relationship with their creator.

The book is best read slowly. The stages in prayer need to be savoured, practised and prayed. So I would suggest that you turn first to Part 1 and pray it step by step. Take it slowly. There is no need to rush on. As Jim Borst reminds us, there is no need to complete all twelve stages on any given day. One section at a time – or one fraction of one step will suffice to nourish the person who is hungry for God.

When you are familiar with this form of prayer, you may find yourself asking certain questions. Some of these may be answered in Part 2 which also needs to be read slowly and thoughtfully preferably after you have spent some time praying the twelve stages from Part 1.

Some people, glancing at the contents of the book might be beguiled into believing that this method of prayer encourages escapism rather than true prayer. They might accuse Jim Borst of encouraging Christians to run away from the cut and thrust of life and to enter into a self-centred stillness which ignores a needy world. I can only say, in defence, that while I have been drawn deeper into the heart of God the Father through using this method of prayer, I have also been turned inside out in the sense that the prayer has challenged and changed my attitudes and priorities, my relationships, my concern for God's world and my life-style. This is inevitable. To pray is to change. To be open to God is to be open to people. To be drawn closer to God is to catch his compassion for his needy world; to be sent back into the world with our sleeves rolled up, ready for action. Bishop

John Taylor expresses this persuasively in *The Go-Between God*: 'The Holy Spirit is the invisible third party who stands between me and the other, making us mutually aware. Supremely and primarily he opens my eyes to Christ. But he also opens my eyes to the brother in Christ, to the fellow man, or the point of need, or the heart-breaking brutality and the equally heart-breaking beauty of the world. He is the giver of that vision without which people perish. We commonly speak about the Holy Spirit as the source of power. But in fact he enables us not by making us supernaturally strong but by opening our eyes.'[1]

You will notice that Jim Borst pleads with his readers to set aside an hour a day for prayer. That may not be possible for the majority of people using this book. But many people are discovering the value of a Quiet Day or Quiet Evening when, with a book at their side, they move away from busyness and hyper-activity and discover the joy of being found and held by God; of soaking up his love. This would be a good time to pray using these stages of prayer.

When we pray in this way over a period of time, the nature of our time of quiet is transformed. Teresa of Avila described it beautifully. We no longer try to water the garden of our life with the little bucket of busy, vocal, active prayer. Instead we irrigate it with the water pipes of the prayer of loving attentiveness described in this book, we find the garden is being further watered by the streams of contemplation running through it and the refreshing, cleansing, heavy rains of oneness with God. We find our prayer gradually becomes more simple yet more effective.

My prayer for users of this book is that the parched places of their lives might be irrigated so that they become like well watered gardens – watered by the refreshing streams of the great prayer-giver, God's Holy Spirit.

Joyce Huggett

Part 1

The Twelve Stages of Prayer

Chapter 1

A Method of Contemplative Prayer

No words can describe, no book can explain what it means to love Jesus. We can only know it from personal experience. When he visits the heart, it is bathed in the light of truth. When his love burns within us, the world loses all its attraction. Those who have tasted Jesus hunger for more. Those who have drunk of him are thirsty for more. But only those who love him are able to fulfil their desires – to know joy in his embrace now and glory later in his kingdom.

One way Christians down the ages have seen, touched, grasped and held God is through the prayer of contemplation or the prayer of loving attentiveness as it is sometimes called. Through this form of prayer they have also been seen, touched and held by God.

There is only one way to practise this kind of prayer and that is by setting aside a regular time and place to pray quietly. As with all forms of prayer there are different stages on the journey into contemplation. I have divided these into twelve steps. Some people find it helpful, in the stillness, to 'dwell in' just one stage. On another occasion, depending on their needs or circumstances, those same people might move from one stage to another.

If you are just starting to pray in this way, you might find it helpful, initially, to spend your prayer time quietly seeking an awareness of the Lord's presence. Then, go through the twelve steps taking one a day. As you become more familiar with them, each day's needs will determine which steps you use and which you omit.

An Overview

Before you begin, it might be helpful to have an overview of the twelve stages of prayer:

1 – 3: Relaxation and Silence. Awareness of God's Presence.
These help us to seek for God and to reach out to him.

4 – 7: Surrender, Acceptance, Forgiving from the Heart and Repentance.
These are concerned with the purification of the heart and mind and help us to become transparent and free before God.

8 – 11: Asking in Faith, Contemplation and Receiving, Thanksgiving and Praise.
These take us to the heart of prayer and enable us to receive from God and to love him.

12: Intercession.
In this last stage, as in all the other stages, we become involved in the prayer in a deeply personal way – with our truest self. We also learn that the Spirit of God breathes as and when he wills; that he encourages us to become pilgrims, always on the move, always more eager to reach the presence of the Lord. And we realise that these twelve steps or suggestions are, indeed, only suggestions.

1. RELAXATION AND SILENCE

This prayer involves a search for peace, tranquillity and serenity. We seek to meet the Lord of the Sabbath in his place of rest deep within us and, as we rest and relax in his presence, to give him the worship of our lives.

A major task, therefore, while we pray, is to let go of tension, to calm down, to accept his will, to surrender to him in faith so that at his word storms may cease. We become alert and attentive, not with a violent effort, but by gently letting go of all tension, excitement, anxiety, worries, the heat of desire, the venom of hatred, the weighing down of self pity.

The word 'concentration' is often used in connection with contemplative prayer. This concentration or attentiveness is not the result of a mighty and tense effort; it is a gentle letting go of things, a relaxing of our nervous grip on people and situations and the release from worry and anxiety.

While all these flow out of us, there remains only one thing: attention to the Lord, awareness of the presence of him who is the author and giver of all peace and strength.

So during this first stage of prayer we just sit down and RELAX.

> SLOWLY AND DELIBERATELY LET ALL TENSION FLOW AWAY. GENTLY SEEK AN AWARENESS OF THE IMMEDIATE AND PERSONAL PRESENCE OF GOD.

There is no violence in this movement: no suppression of moods, feelings, frustrations. Suppression implies violence and increases tension. Just relax and let go of everything as you enter into the awareness of God's presence.

We can relax and let go of everything precisely *because* God

is present. In his presence nothing really matters; all things are in his hands. Tension, anxiety, worry, frustration, all melt away before him, as snow before the sun.

Some people find it helpful in this first stage of prayer to listen to quiet music[1] and to become aware of their breathing. Tension, worry and excitement lead to short, shallow breathing. Making our breathing slower and a little deeper helps us to relax and to enjoy a greater sense of peace and serenity. Since God invites us to 'be still and know that I am God' (Ps. 46:10) and since Jesus invites those who are weary to come to him and rest, it can help, as we breathe in to say the word 'Be' and, as we breathe out, to say the word 'still'. Gradually, we find ourselves not only saying, 'Be still', we are actually becoming still. As we say the words 'come … rest', we find ourselves responding to that invitation and actually resting.

> NEXT SEEK PEACE AND INNER SILENCE. LET YOUR MIND, HEART, WILL AND FEELINGS BECOME TRANQUIL AND SERENE. LET INNER STORMS SUBSIDE: OBSESSIONAL THOUGHTS, PASSIONATE DRIVES OF WILL AND EMOTIONS. 'SEEK PEACE, AND PURSUE IT.' (Ps. 34:14)

Be ready, if necessary, to spend all your prayer time like this, without any thought of result, effect or reward. Be prepared to 'waste' time; to make it a naked, selfless offering of time and attention for God alone.

This movement towards peace and silence opens us to an inflow of grace; it creates a condition in which a genuine, true, and personal love for God to be awakened within. It can be sustained by continuing to be aware of our breathing and by saying the name Jesus: 'Je' as we breathe in and 'sus' as we breathe out. This movement becomes an act of surrender; an acceptance of God's will. We make it possible for the heart, will, and emotions to become impregnated with God's gift of peace and with his will.

Although some people find that relaxing in this way coupled with quiet breathing makes them fall asleep, the aim is to relax in order to be awake and alert to the presence of God; to become rather like sentries who make themselves quiet in order to listen for the presence of others or to become like a mother whose ear is always listening for the faintest whimper of her new-born baby The mind, nerves, and emotions are stilled so that the heart may be ready. In the words of the Psalmist:

'Oh God, my heart is ready to praise you!
I will sing and rejoice before you.' (Ps. 108:1)

2. AWARENESS OF GOD'S PRESENCE

Open yourself to an awareness of God's presence.

He is present to your spirit and attentive to your awareness of him. He dwells in the core of your being. Today you seek an awareness of this, but one day he will give you this awareness freely.

He is closer to your true self than you are to yourself. He knows you better than you know yourself. He loves you better than you love yourself. He is 'Abba. Father, to you. YOU ARE because HE IS.

In the mirror of created existence, you are his living image and likeness:

- when you know, you reflect his knowledge;
- when you love, you reflect his love;
- when you call out to him, he hears;
- when you seek his awareness,
  he awakens you to his presence
  in and through and with Jesus.

HE SPEAKS HIS WORD OF LOVE:

'YOU ARE MY SON,
YOU ARE MY DAUGHTER,
BELOVED OF ME,
IN WHOM I AM WELL PLEASED.'

In and through and with Jesus, he pours out his Spirit, making you call out, 'Abba, Father'. He fills you with thanks and praise for his wonderful presence.

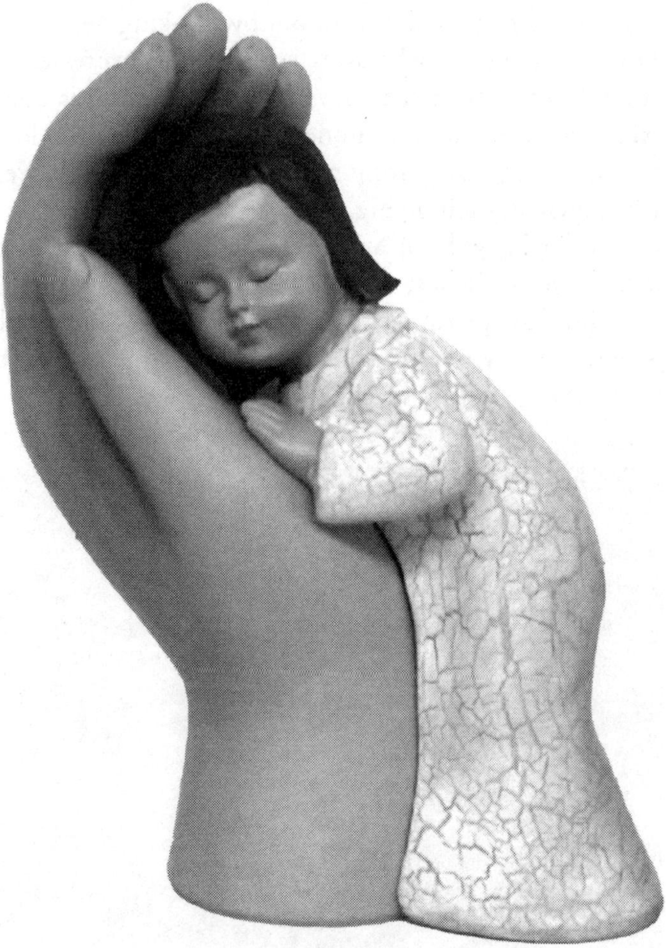

3. LONGING LOVE

The author of *The Cloud of Unknowing* once claimed: 'By love he can be caught and held, but by thinking never.'[2]

Love for someone who is as yet absent is expressed in a mixture of love and desire. Love for someone who is present is expressed through communication: receiving their loving presence, giving love from our hearts, expressing love in words, touch and self-giving.

So we begin with an awareness of the emptiness of our hearts. Then, in silence, we seek God with longing, reaching out to him. The picture is that of a person who, in complete darkness, reaches out to the loved one who is somewhere present, nearby, within reach.

It is the heart that reaches out (hands tend to express what is in the heart); it is not the mind that can touch him. The mind thinks and reflects about a person in their absence; as soon as the person enters, the mind stops thinking about him; instead there is a communication of presence; a giving and taking in of the reality of one another. 'He may well be loved, but not thought.'[3]

We can express our longing love in two ways which go together:

1. By a slow, deep, rhythmic breathing. As we breathe in, we breathe in his loving presence; after holding that breath for one or two seconds, we breathe our slowly but fully all that is not him. We can spend all our prayer time in this way if necessary.

2. By calling his name repeatedly – saying the name 'Jesus' or 'Abba' or 'Father'. This is not a mechanical repetition of sounds, like saying a mantra, it is a loving heart-cry. The focus of our mind and heart, as much as possible, is God. That is why it is best to use the name of Jesus or Abba or Father. When we begin this Jesus Prayer or Father Prayer a number of things might happen. Initially, we simply repeat the sounds with our lips (vocal prayer). After some time, we begin repeating the words mentally, while the lips might be still (mental prayer). Gradually we may find ourselves repeating the name in our heart. At this stage we know that our heart has awakened and has begun to pray. The prayer has descended from the head into the heart. And when the heart has begun to pray there is an inflow of grace by which we know God in our heart in a new way.

4. SURRENDER

Spending time surrendering ourselves to God is one way of fulfilling his commandment: 'You must love the Lord your God with all your heart, and all your soul and all your strength and all your mind' (Matt. 22:37). Our way of loving him lies in surrendering each and every part of ourselves to him and in seeking to be loved and filled by him. The Seventh Day (the Sabbath) was originally instituted so that we should have adequate time to give him our loving attention, and surrender ourselves to him.

Before God's face, aware of his presence,
SURRENDER EVERY ASPECT OF YOUR BEING:
your hands, your wrists, your arms;
your senses and brain;
your feet and legs;
each and every nerve and muscle, blood vessel and organ.

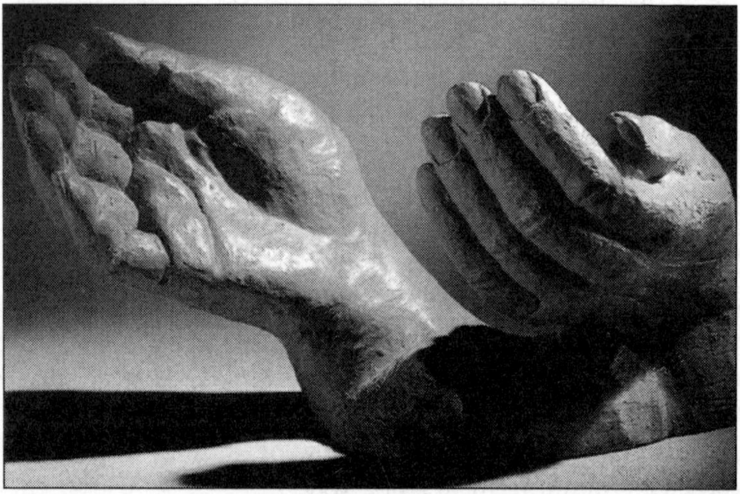

Return yourself to him. Seek to withdraw your possessiveness and beg him to possess you, to live in and through you so that you can say with Paul: 'I no longer live, but Christ lives in me' (Gal. 2:20). Ask him to accept every part of you, to make of you an instrument of peace.

SURRENDER YOUR CARES AND WORRIES ...
Gradually we grow in an awareness that if our faith and hope in him are true, there is no ground for anxiety and tension; he takes care of and looks after his sons and daughters. So we let go of everything that preoccupies us in a movement of faith and surrender. From now on we let him lead us step by step.

SURRENDER YOUR HEART, YOUR FEELINGS, YOUR LOVE ...
The heart does not love with its own love. 'Whoever loves is a child of God and knows God' (1 Jn. 4:7). It is Jesus who through his Spirit loves his Father in 'our' breath of love. It is not we who love but he who loves in us and through us. And his love is quiet, serene, ineffable and enduring.

SURRENDER YOUR WHOLE PERSONALITY, YOUR FEELINGS AND ALL THAT IS 'YOU' ...

> Grope towards a gentle love, beyond thinking,
> 'towards where One waited near,
> Whose Presence well I knew,
> there where no other might appear,'[4]

5. Acceptance

May of our 'natural' reactions are expressions and gestures of non-acceptance, of rebellion, of running away from reality, of suppression. Anger flares up; impatience possesses us like an evil spirit; dislikes and grudges harden our hearts; we resent interference and interruption. Without always realising it, we often refuse to accept people, events, situations, conditions, even ourselves as God wills them for us and as he accepts them for us.

This non-acceptance of his will in concrete circumstances is experienced in prayer as a barrier, a road-block on the way to God. It is his will that we accept people, circumstances, events; that we do not try to influence people or events except by the power of love, forgiveness, suffering, acceptance and thanksgiving. In daily life, this means that we seek to avoid being judgemental, argumentative, critical and interfering in matters that do not concern us.

ASK GOD TO MAKE YOU AWARE OF ACTUAL BARRIERS OF NON-ACCEPTANCE IN YOUR LIFE.

Look at each barrier and deliberately accept God's will in this matter. Withdraw any self-oriented and condemnatory judgement. Withhold any criticism. Repent of any violent thoughts, words and deeds. Risk the leap of faith and love and turn your heart towards him who makes all things work for good for those who love him (Rom. 8:28).

Acceptance of God's will is identical with acceptance of his guidance and lordship. As he leads us, step by step, through the concrete circumstances of our daily lives, he guides and leads us into his Kingdom. His Kingdom is advanced whenever we accept and do his will.

Lay down your will and try to discern God's will.

Thoughts and plans lose their compulsion as we seek to see his plan unfolding and as we endeavour to follow his pattern and call.

6. FORGIVING FROM THE HEART

The God whom we seek is full of compassion and forgiveness. Even before we repent and seek his mercy, his forgiveness is ready, waiting for us. Our heavenly Father calls us to be like him, as true sons and daughters. Jesus, his Beloved Son, manifested true Sonship in that he freely forgave and loved those who hurt him: Father forgive them, for they do not know what they are doing' (Luke 23:34).

Few things close our hearts to God's grace and to his loving presence as much as resentment, lack of forgiveness and hurt feelings. Our hearts have been created for loving, from deep within ourselves to be channels of his love. Resentment and lack of forgiveness block and poison our hearts. Yet God says through the Psalmist: 'Harden not your hearts ...'

The first step, when we detect the hardening of the heart, is to forgive the one who has hurt us. This decision is almost always an act of the will. But more is needed. Our hearts need to be cleansed of bitterness and healed of hurt and pain, so that we can remember whatever has happened with undisturbed inner peace.

The best way to come to this deeper cleansing and healing, as we come before the Lord, is to close our eyes, and recall the memory: re-entering the situation by visualising the place and person(s) who were present at the time. Next, imagine Jesus himself coming to you in that place and at the time when the incident occurred. He was there then but you may not have noticed him. Notice him now. What does he want to do for you? How does he want to express the love which is in his heart for you?

Among other things, he will eventually ask you to forgive the other person(s). So, when you are ready, address that

person saying something like: 'In Jesus' Name, I forgive you from my heart.'

Continue to pray like this until you can 'see' the Lord loving that person and until you are able to love and accept that person also.

When there is a deep hurt, you may need to spend all your time of prayer working on his one memory-relationship. But it is worth it.

On another occasion, you may like to make a list of between three and eight people you have disliked from childhood onwards. Beginning with the first, pray in the way I have described. Pray for each person on the list individually. This will open your innermost being to the grace of contemplative prayer.

7. Repentance and Forgiveness

When we enter this stage, we may be oppressed by a sense of sin and failure. It may be a general sense of sin and unworthiness, or it may arise because of a particular situation. We must face this barrier in a spirit of genuine repentance and true humility.

Confess your sins and failings and beg God's forgiveness, thanking him for hearing your prayer.

Then face him as you are: sinful, spiritually handicapped and disabled in many ways; a chronic patient. Accept these handicaps and disabilities because he accepts you as you are and loves you as you are.

Refuse to nurse a sense of guilt. Instead, embrace God's forgiveness and love.

Guilt and inferiority feelings before God can be expressions of selfishness or self-centredness; a sign that we are giving greater importance to our little sinful selves than to his immense and never-ending love.

Surrender your guilt and inferiority to God.

His goodness is greater than your badness. Accept his joy in loving and forgiving you. It is a healing grace to surrender your sinfulness to his mercy.

You may want to spend some time letting all this sink into your consciousness.

REPENTANCE

When we find ourselves unable to pray for no precise reason except a sense of unease and unworthiness, some advice given in *The Cloud of Unknowing* may help:

'When we repent, we should simply use the word 'sin' without analysing what kind it is: Pride, anger, envy, avarice, sloth, gluttony or lust. What does it matter to contemplatives what sort of sin it is, or how great? When they are engaged in contemplation, they think all sins are great since the smallest sin seems to separate them from God and prevents spiritual peace.

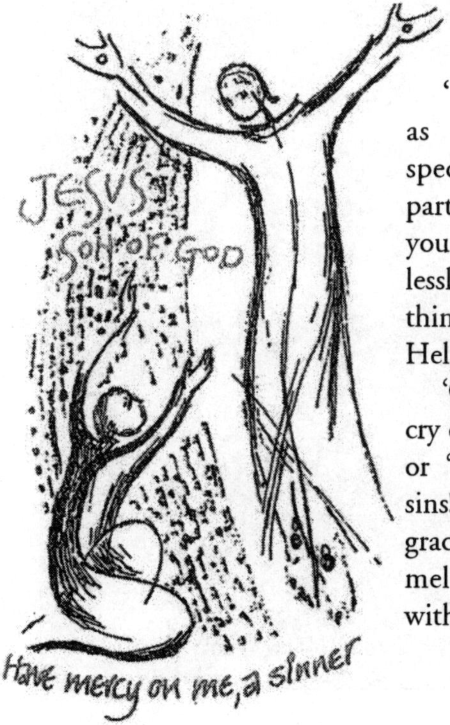

'**Feel sin in its totality** – as a lump – without specifying any particular part, and that all of it is you. And then cry ceaselessly in your spirit this one thing: "Sin! Sin! Sin! Help! Help! Help!"

'One may also repeatedly cry out "Lord, have mercy!" or "Jesus, forgive me my sins!" until He gives the grace of compunction and melts the lump of sin within us.[5]

8. Asking in Faith

Prayer is not something we do on our own. When we take one step towards him, God moves towards us. There are two steps which hasten his coming in grace. One is the step of accepting (at a definite time and place) Jesus as your *personal*

Lord and Saviour. This involves an acceptance of him and a yielding to him at a very deep and personal level. He always responds to this acceptance, which enables him to begin to manifest his lordship and saving power. The second step is to pray that, in the silence, God will touch you afresh through his Spirit. Beg for the Spirit's out-pouring, for a personal anointing, for his gifts and for a sense of his presence and peace at the core of your being:

> Come, Holy Spirit,.
> fill my heart, now surrendered to Jesus,
> my Saviour and Lord.
> Enkindle in me the fire of divine love.
> Fill me with the glorious presence of my Risen Lord,
> so that it may no longer be I who live
> but he who lives in me.

Ask that he may live and reign in you. Surrender yourself to Jesus, your Saviour and accept him as Lord. He has prayed and suffered to free you and claim you as his own.

Say to him:

> Take me and all I have,
> do with me whatever you will.
> Send me where you will.
> Use me as you will.
> I surrender myself and all I possess
> absolutely and entirely,
> unconditionally and forever
> to your control.

9. Contemplation

By now you have put away all obstacles from your heart, all wavering from your will. Now you can say with the unknown author of *The Cloud of Unknowing*: 'Him I covet, Him I seek and nothing but Him.'[6]

'It is enough that I should feel moved lovingly by I know now what, and that in this inward urge I have no real thought for anything less than God, and that my desire is steadily and simply turned towards Him.'[7]

'I lift up my heart to God with humble love. And I really mean *God Himself* who created me, and bought me and graciously calls me – and not what I get out of Him. Indeed, I hate to think of anything but God Himself, so that nothing occupies my mind or will but only God … I think no other thought of Him, apart from my awareness of Him darkly but gloriously present. It all depends on my desire: a naked intention directed to God, and himself alone.'[8]

I turn myself entirely to his presence. I look steadily at him. His presence becomes more real to me. He holds my inward sight. My glance simply and lovingly rests on him. My prayer is nothing but a loving awareness of him. 'I look because I love; I look in order to love, and my love is fed and influenced by looking.'[9]

10. Receiving

God always responds. He cannot refuse a seeking in faith and love. 'Seek and you will find' becomes 'Seek and you will always be found.' He seeks you before you seek him, while you seek him and after you have sought him. As God himself puts it, 'I have loved you with an everlasting love, so I am constant in my affection for you!' (Jer. 31:3)

He responds. He turns to you. He seeks you. He is anxious to invade your spirit. He wants his Spirit to possess you. You bask in the warmth of his love. You feel his gaze upon you. Jesus, your Lord, is eager to possess your heart, to love his Father with it and to radiate his love from it. As Jesus put it:

> 'Anyone who loves me will keep my word,
> and my Father will love him,
> and we shall come to him
> and make our home in him.' (John 14:23 JB)

God fills you with his presence and his Spirit. It is only by his grace or through faith that you may discern and experience him.

His presence brings a deep, spiritual peace; a share in his Sabbath rest, a greater serenity, a welling up of joy and love, a flood of grace, a strong desire to praise and thank him.

Or, if it be his will, his presence brings the power to serve him and proclaim him. To bear witness to his kingdom, to bring healing in his name, to bring peace and unity to people of goodwill.

You experience for yourself John's claim:

'We have recognised for ourselves,
and put our faith in the love God has for us.
God is love,
and whoever remains in love remains in God
and God in him.' (1 John 4:16 JB)

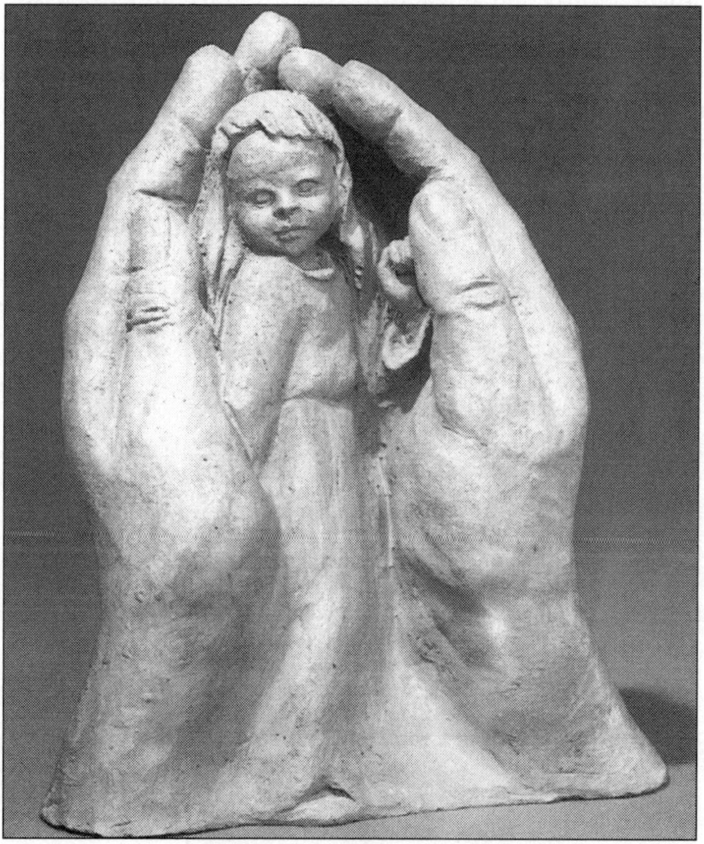

11. PRAISE AND THANKSGIVING

Jesus invariably thanked and praised his Father and taught his disciples to do the same. The prayer of Jesus recorded in John 17 is one of praise, thanksgiving and intercession.

When he has made his presence known or touched you with his Spirit and filled you with his grace and peace, you will spontaneously begin to thank and praise him.

And the time may well come when you begin to thank him for the privilege of sharing in the loneliness and suffering of Jesus simply because his will is being done in you.

12. Intercession

You may want to spend some time in intercession at the end of your period of prayer. Intercessory prayer is important. That is why Jesus continues to intercede for you unceasingly (see Heb. 7:25) and in addition to his own prayer, he needs to intercede through your heart. He wants to pray and suffer through you.

So you must plead with simple and expectant faith and lever lose heart (Luke 18:1). Believe his promise: 'Ask and you will always receive.' Learn to pray as the Lord has urged: with faith that he has already given what you ask for (Mark 11:24). Pray, according to his will, for his Kingdom in yourself and others.

Lord,
teach me how to pray;
glorify your Name;
your Kingdom come;
your will be done in my life
and the life of others.
Grant your peace to …
Help … in his (her) need.
Make your love known to …

Part 2

Some Questions Answered

Chapter 2

What is Contemplation?

If you have been experimenting with the steps or stages of prayer outlined in Part 1 of this book, you may be asking yourself the question: What is contemplation? Or maybe others are asking you that question?

It may best be answered by taking a look at the three classical stages of prayer.

Vocal Prayer

First, there is vocal prayer: a prayer of the lips, with stress on words, recited or sung. The text may be ready-made like the Lord's Prayer. Often it is beautiful and inspiring. Vocal prayer may also be *spontaneous*, talking to God in our own words as we would talk to a friend.

Meditative Prayer

Then, there is meditative prayer or meditation when the lips are quiet but the mind is active: picturing, pondering, reflecting and thinking about God and his wonderful dealings. The mind seeks understanding and insight. In meditation we might take a passage from the Gospels, put ourselves into the scene and ask what Jesus is doing and saying to us.

CONTEMPLATIVE PRAYER

Finally, there is Contemplative Prayer or contemplation: a prayer of heart and will which reaches out to God's presence. The lips and mind both come to rest: there is a simple gazing at the Lord while the heart reaches out without words and the will seeks to be one with God's will. As one author has put it: Contemplation is 'the awareness of God, known and loved at the core of one's being.'[10]

If we compare contemplative prayer to vocal prayer, it could be said that in contemplative prayer we seek an awareness that what is contained in the words 'is really and truly present to us.' In praying the words, 'our Father in heaven', for example, we go beyond the words to an awareness of God's presence deep within us and dwell in that presence. The actual words become rather like the ringing of a bell awakening us from sleep to a consciousness of Christ's indwelling presence.

In comparing contemplative prayer to meditative prayer, we could say that, in contemplative prayer, instead of mulling over the truth reflectively, we come to a halt and gaze at it, becoming aware that God is living in us. While meditation may be compared to the activity that goes into making and painting a picture, contemplation is more like the quiet looking at the completed picture, seeing it as a whole, becoming aware of the reality of the artist's vision which it portrays.

In contemplation, we go beyond symbols (words, thoughts, concepts), so that we may enter a reality which is spiritual and true, enduring and over-powering. This reality is God: Father, Son and Holy Spirit. Since this reality is beyond the compass of clear concepts and beyond description of any kind, our minds cannot see or grasp it. But love can discern it and the Holy Spirit awakens this love. As the author of *The Cloud of Unknowing* expresses it, 'Though we cannot know him we can love him. By love may he be touched and embraced, never by thought.'[11]

The Lord may graciously return this love and so John of the Cross writing in sixteenth century Spain can say, 'Contemplation is nothing else but a secret, peaceful infusion of God, which, if admitted, will set the soul on fire with the Spirit of love.'[12]

THE TWO STAGES OF CONTEMPLATIVE PRAYER

Contemplative prayer has two stages. The first is usually known as ACQUIRED CONTEMPLATION when, in faith, hope and with a longing love, we reach out to God's presence. It begins with knowing in faith that he is really present and seeking with all one's heart to touch him and be touched by him.

The second is INFUSED CONTEMPLATION when, through his grace, as a free gift, God gives us a real awareness of his presence. This may come through a whole variety of ways: through experiencing the fruits of the Spirit, for example: love, joy, peace: through a heart-assurance that he is present to us or in some other way.

I used to wonder whether infused contemplation was only for some gifted individuals or whether it was for everyone. I found my answer in the words of Jesus who said: 'Keep on asking and you will receive. Keep on seeking and you will find. Keep on knocking and the door will be opened to you.'[13]

The Prayer of the Heart

Contemplative prayer is the prayer of the heart. It could be argued that we all have two hearts: the physical heart which is the vital organ situated left of centre in the chest and a spiritual heart which is the centre of our self-identity; of the spiritual dimension of our being.

When we refer to ourselves, we frequently point to the centre of our chest as though aware that this is where the real 'me', the core of my being, my deepest self, is located. It may be that when we pray, 'Come into my heart Lord Jesus', or when we invite the Risen Lord into our hearts we picture him dwelling in this part of our anatomy.

But the spiritual heart cannot be pin-pointed so easily. Perhaps that is why many people are only vaguely aware that they have such a thing. They may experience the spiritual heart only as a centre of emotions: love, joy, sorrow, anger, peace, fear, loneliness, pain. Yet this heart has deeper layers of self-awareness which can be opened to others – especially to God. This inner heart has been created to become his dwelling place. Here he dwells by grace as the source of the spring of living water, as the source of true love.

This prayer of the heart springs from the other kinds of prayer. In fact, the three stages of prayer may be compared to stages of schooling. We begin in primary school with reading and writing to which we compare vocal prayer. We continue in middle school which, in prayer, means meditation, where reflection on life and revelation is the main subject, although vocal prayer is not neglected. The high school of prayer is the beginning of the prayer recommended here: contemplation. We do not forget or neglect what we have learned already; but the growing point is an awakening to God's presence and an opening to his Spirit. Mature Christians are encouraged to explore contemplative prayer. Such maturity can be reached in one's teens or much later and this form of prayer is available to young or old, singles or marrieds.

Charismatic Prayer

Contemplative prayer opens us to the activity and gifts of God's Spirit and to his cleansing and healing action. For this reason contemplative prayer may also be described as charismatic prayer – and vice versa. In silent prayer, as in charismatic prayer, there is a movement towards complete surrender to the indwelling Holy Spirit of God; the helper Jesus promised when he said: 'I will ask the Father, and he will give you another helper, who will stay with you forever' (John 14:16). In contemplative prayer as in charismatic prayer, there is also the realisation that the helper who will stay with us for ever will also supply us with all the spiritual gifts we need.

This helper journeys alongside us to the mountain of the Lord. Although we begin the pilgrimage on our own two feet, it is the breath of God's Spirit which carries us forward and upward. There are maps and guides. And on the journey, we meet people who can encourage and help us. But it is the glory of the Lord dimly seen at the end of the journey that draw us, to quote C.S. Lewis, 'further up and further in.'[14]

Chapter 3

Why Practise Contemplative Prayer?

A frequent question about contemplative prayer is, 'Why do you want to pray in this way?' There are different ways of answering. One possibility is to say that contemplative prayer lies at the heart of the gospel and at the heart of the Christian life. A careful study of the Bible illustrates this. We see that there contemplative prayer was the prayer of the prophets as well as of the ordinary people of the Old Testament who endeavoured to love God with all their heart, with all their soul, with all their mind and with all their strength (Deut. 6:5) and to worship in the contemplative peace and rest of the Sabbath.

Contemplative prayer was also the prayer of Jesus. This is the main reason why many Christians today and throughout the ages have found themselves compelled to pursue the contemplative path.

The Gospel writers reveal that, alongside his active, public life, Jesus sought to live a life of solitude, privacy, silence, fasting and watching, listening and prayer. In the silence he learned to know his Father's will and experienced complete surrender in love. In the silence he heard his Father speak: 'This is my Son, whom I have chosen – listen to him!' (Luke 9:35) In the silence he knew his Father in love (John 10:15). Jesus experienced this oneness with God in and through his human nature, which was in every way like our own, with the exception of sin. 'We all know he did not come as an angel but as a human being … like us … though he never sinned.' (Hebrews 2:16 and 4:15 LB).

Jesus wants us to share in his own experience of kinship with the Father in the love of the Spirit: 'for from the very beginning God decided that those who came to him … should become like his Son, so that his Son would be the First, with many brothers' (Rom. 8:29 LB). By sharing his Spirit of love and surrender with his disciples, Jesus made this possible. In contemplative prayer, in a very imperfect and faltering manner, we recreate and experience the oneness Jesus enjoyed with the Father. In addition, contemplative prayer is one of the ways in which we may behold God's glory (1 Cor. 13:12; 1 John 3:2).

THE PRAYER THAT TRANSFORMS US

We may find ourselves drawn to contemplative prayer because it is life-changing.

My experience is that the fruits and benefits of a daily discipline of contemplative prayer are given, not so much during the time of silence as afterwards when prayer affects the quality of one's life.

During the time of prayer, I often have a sense that I am wasting my time or I may be distracted or sleepy. Yet the act of seeking God with my whole heart and will and the grace-filled effects of his actual presence draw me deeper and deeper into him.

Outside my prayer time, I find that I spontaneously remember his presence more frequently. It may be a moment when I thank him or when I whisper, 'I love you.' I also become aware of a deeper peace filling me. I can work better and cope more successfully with people and things. I am eager to serve God more effectively and to do only what he asks of me. What counts is not what pleases me but what God asks of me. In other words, this daily prayer is transforming my entire life.

This is the effect of contemplative prayer. True spirituality and true prayer must change us, otherwise they are irrelevant and scandalous. We cannot pray day after day, month after month and remain the same. If we do not change in any way, our seeking and prayer are not genuine but a subtle way of keeping the Spirit from intruding into our lives.

Real contemplative prayer involves an opening to the Spirit. His gifts and his fruits will be more and more in evidence. We may not necessarily be aware of the way in which prayer is changing us and for this reason it can be important to have a 'soul friend' or spiritual guide to help us to see whether we really are changing, however slightly and slowly. It should also be said that as we enter into contemplative prayer we can receive the impression that we are going backwards instead of making progress! The reason for this is that, sometimes, as the light of God enters into us we 'see' imperfections and faults in ourselves for the first time. They may have been there for months or years but we did not see them until we entered into a deeper form of prayer. Far from going backwards, this is a sign of progress but it is another reason why we may need a guide or 'soul friend' to journey with us along the path of prayer.

As we journey on, we shall become more and more aware of Jesus' personal gift to us; his peace. We shall also find ourselves being healed in the living water of his Spirit and we shall grow more like Jesus.

The author of the medieval treatise on contemplation *The Cloud of Unknowing*, described this transformation in a delightful manner.

> 'All who engage in this work of contemplation find that it has a good effect on the body as well as on the soul, for it makes them attractive in the eyes of all who see them. So much so that the ugliest person alive who becomes, by grace, a contemplative finds that he suddenly, (and again by grace) is different, and that every good man he sees is glad and happy to have his friendship, and is spiritually refreshed, and helped nearer God by his company.
>
> Therefore, seek to get this gift by grace; for whoever really has it will be well able to control both himself and his possessions by virtue of it. It gives him discernment, when he needs it, to read people's needs and characters. It gives him a knack of being at home with every one he talks to, habitual sinner or not, without sinning himself ... to the astonishment of the onlooker, and with a magnetic effect on others, drawing them by grace to the same spiritual work that he practices. His face and his words are full of spiritual wisdom, fervent and fruitful, assured and free from

falsehood, far from feigned and affected "hypocrites"'.[15]

The author goes on to make the point that those who have learned to be relaxed, outgoing, and at ease with God behave in the same way towards other people. We love to be with a person who radiates such peace and strength. And we love to be with a person who is sympathetic and sensitive towards us whereas those who are nervous, irritable or angry are most unpleasant company.

Teresa of Avila testified to the effectiveness of contemplative prayer when she said: 'If you will try and live in the presence of God for one year, you will see yourself at the end of it at the height of perfection, yet without realising it.'

A more recent testimony claims something similar:

'After less than two years serious effort in contemplative prayer, I recognise that the following changes have taken place in me:

Joy, peace, calm now reign where before there was fear, tension, unrest of all kinds. Even in difficult situations and decisions, peace remains and solutions are brought about in most unexpected ways – not products of my own wisdom, they just seem to happen without my knowing how.

A growing conviction of the reality that is God and of his Spirit, glimpses of the Fatherhood of God, a sense of personal dignity and worth because of his personal love for me have replaced former self-hatred and negativism.

I am now able peacefully to accept my work

including its unpleasant duties and the criticism which comes and I have more tolerance and am able to accept others with less irritability. Given my proud temperament and nature, I see that, through God's mercy, I have been prevented from many tragedies. Through a gradual discovery of my false humility I now have a real desire for truth. Many psychological disorders have come to light making me more free.

There is a greater appreciation of the *gift* of vocation and more stability and genuineness in striving to live it. Other prayers and devotions are more meaningful. Desire for God has grown. This gives me more courage in the striving; whereas formerly I was given to despondency and self-pity.

I think it is true that faith, hope and love have been deepened. I long to share this treasure.'

The Prayer that sets us Free

Another wholesome effect or fruit of this prayer is that, through the action of the Holy Spirit, we become more fully and more truly human.

In the presence of God, we learn the necessity of being absolutely true to ourselves and absolutely honest with ourselves. We learn to see ourselves as we really are – behind the mask of convention and deception, pose and pretence. We grow into truthfulness and genuineness as we grow out of artificiality and falseness in thought, word and deed. The more we live in the presence of God, the more truly we become ourselves – the people God always intended us to be.

And as we become more true to ourselves, we become more true to God, to the people we live with and to our surroundings. We become more objective in our search for knowledge and in the way we evaluate the information we have. Our capacity for genuine personal relationship increases and we grow in our ability to enter with empathy and compassion into the feelings, situations and needs of other people. All this accompanies contemplative prayer which is the ability to be open to God and to ourselves.

The Prayer that Transforms our Spirituality

Contemplative prayer brings a new meaning and sense of unity to other types of prayer. We may begin to move away from a 'routine' way of praying which follows a set pattern. All prayers begin to take on a contemplative quality, to become real and deep. Initially, there may be an inability to tolerate any prayer that is said hurriedly or inattentively and without due reverence for the meaning of the words. And we may find it necessary to use fewer set prayers. At another stage we may return to such prayers, especially those of a repetitive kind like The Lord's Prayer and The Jesus Prayer because these help us to dwell in the presence of God and to 'wander with him'.

Contemplative prayer further transforms other kinds of prayer because it leads us into a state of 'God-realisation'. As, single-mindedly, we seek God's presence, we experience him in our hearts. We know him, are filled with him and become more and more one with him – especially in the stillness.

Chapter 4

What Does Contemplation Achieve?

In addition to the fruits of contemplation which I outlined under the question, *Why practise contemplation*? I would like to highlight three other results of contemplative prayer.

Contemplation Overcomes Weakness

The first is the effect it has on our *faults and weaknesses.* We all have them. And, in spite of our good intentions, we find ourselves powerless to overcome them: criticism, impatience, loss of temper, harsh words, grudges, to mention a few.

These faults disrupt our peace with others, with ourselves and with God. But when we seek God in the stillness and surrender to him through contemplative prayer, our weaknesses lose some of their power over us. As *The Cloud of Unknowing* tells us: 'In contemplation a soul dries up the root and ground of sin that is always there, even after one's confession, and however busy one is in holy things.'[16]

That is not to say that such faults disappear immediately.

On the contrary, there sometimes seems to be no marked improvement for some considerable time. But God *is* remoulding us. And provided we are genuinely making every effort to change, we are becoming like soft clay in his hands. We may not see the changes he is making because he wants us to recognise our dependency on him. We will only know that we are being changed when others tell us that we are behaving differently.

Contemplation Reduces Tension

The second benefit of contemplative prayer is that it can help to reduce *tension and nervousness.* This is of special importance to people living in community and to families because of the constant need to be available and open to other community or family members. Because contemplative prayer persuades us to seek peace, love and non-violence in our attitudes and our actions, it can be a useful tool in helping to make or mend relationships and it is more productive than confrontation.

Contemplation Brings Balance

The third effect of contemplation is to bring balance and healing into our lives. We all need a daily rhythm of sleep and wakefulness, work and relaxation, food and exercise. We all need rest and a regular period of contemplative prayer enables us to rest in the love of God.

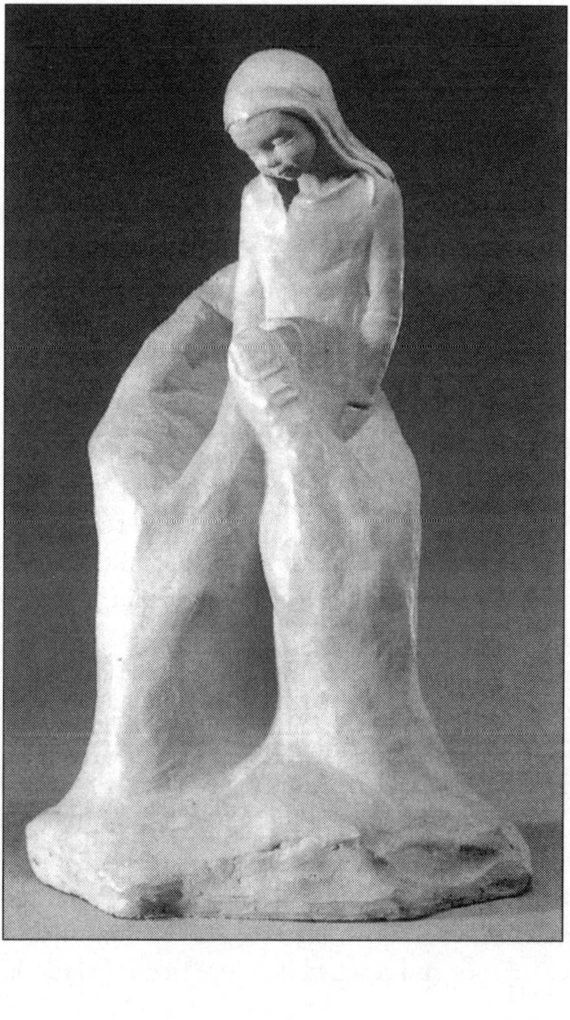

Chapter 5

Where Should I Pray?

If at all possible, find a place which is completely private, where there is not too much noise and where you are unlikely to be disturbed. Trying to pray in the same room with others may be difficult because the awareness of their presence can be a powerful psychological distraction and a hindrance to complete relaxation.

Jesus says, 'Whenever you pray, go to your room, close your door, and pray to your Father in private' (Matt 6:6). He himself 'often retired to deserted places and prayed' (Luke 5:16). But we may take comfort from the fact that he did not always succeed in getting away: 'Then he said to hem, "You must come away to some lonely place all by yourselves and rest for a while" ... but people saw them going and many could guess where; and from every town they all hurried to the place on foot and reached it before them' (Mark 6:30-33).

Chapter 6

How Long Should I Pray?

If it is at all possible, give yourself a full hour for prayer. If that sounds a long time, remember that one full hour a day represents about four percent of an average life-time. At first, it may seem a very long time and you may find that praying for an hour needs perseverance and an agonising effort. But gradually, one learns to value this leisurely time spent with and for God.

Not everyone will be able to manage an hour at a stretch. You may have young children or an elderly relative to look after, for example. Decide how long is realistic for you and be as faithful as possible in sticking to that time.

If, in the middle of your prayer time, something unavoidable happens: the baby wakes up, your elderly relative really needs you, then, of course you must leave your place of prayer. If this happens ask the Holy Spirit to finish the prayer for you. But try not to give up on prayer simply because nothing seems to be happening. Prayer has been described as 'wasting time' with God and we are sometimes more conscious of time-wasting than of the presence of God.

The author of *The Cloud of Unknowing* encourages us to make the necessary effort: 'Work hard at it … and take your rest later! It is hard work and no mistake, for the would-be contemplative; very hard work indeed unless it is made easier by special grace of God or by the fact that one has got used to it over a long period.'[17]

If you are unable to spend an hour in prayer every day, try to carve out a full hour once a week or even once a month. You will usually find that this hour gives you time to unwind, to relax and to focus so fully on Jesus that you are able to receive whatever he wants to give you. If your time of prayer is too short, you will spend most of it unwinding. Just as you are ready to start the prayer of contemplation it is time to stop. That is why two separate periods of thirty minutes each is less desirable than the full hour.

It has been said that: 'silence is to the heart what sleep is to the body – nourishment and refreshment.' The more active and distracting our lives, the greater the need for a full hour of relaxation before God. Our need for the steadying, healing impact of this exercise on our nerves and emotions is urgent. Through silent prayer God changes us and renews us more thoroughly then in any other way.

Chapter 7

When Should I Pray?

The time of day *when* we pray depends on other commitments and the demands of family or single life. Some people like the early morning and Jesus seems to have been one of them: 'Rising early the next morning, he went off to a lonely place in the desert; where he was absorbed in prayer' (Mark 1:35). The morning quiet may be rewarding if you are physically and mentally awake then.

Others prefer to pray in the evening before sleep when they find it easier to relax for an hour with Christ.

Many people have no choice and just have to take an hour whenever they can find it. For some, an hour of prayer means giving up things they like to do, while others have to take their time of quiet on a long-distance bus, in an airport or on the commuter train.

Chapter 8

How Do I Deal With Distractions?

Wandering thoughts or distractions are often a problem. How can we deal with them?

If you are unable to relax or unwind, it may be because you are very tired. The first thing is to accept this and to remember that contemplative prayer is for God and not for our own satisfaction. God knows that we want to spend time with him and accepts our loving intention to be with him no matter how feeble our attempts to pray. Be ready to 'waste' part of the time as a sacrifice made for God.

There is a sense in which awareness of failure and sin can help rather than hinder prayer. To feel wholly dependent on God's undeserved love is the best possible preparation for prayer. It means that we have confidence in nothing but God and this opens us up to his peace.

When we continue to seek the presence of God without experiencing that presence and when we continue to love him although he seems to hide himself, we are telling him that our deepest desire is for him and not for anything that he can give us. We long for the Giver more than for his gifts.

However there are specific ways of minimising distractions and keeping our awareness focussed on the presence of God to the greatest possible extent. Here I mention four:

Breathing

Tension, worry and excitement all lead to short and shallow breathing. When we make our breathing more deliberate, slow and regular, tension ebbs away and we become more relaxed and have a greater sense of peace and serenity.

While you pray, try to breathe more slowly and deliberately; deepening your breathing and allowing it to keep in time with your pulse or your heartbeat. It might help if, as you breathe in, you count 1, 2, 3, 4 … up to about 6 to the speed of your heartbeat. This will feel artificial and strange for a while but will become natural as you practise it. Breathe out in the same controlled, slow manner. You can practise this rhythmic breathing at odd times during the day – while walking, sitting quietly or lying down. It is one way of dealing with distractions in prayer.

Repetitive Prayers

Rhythmic breathing can be accompanied by repetitive prayer in an attempt to deal with distractions. One of the best known repetitive prayers is the Jesus Prayer. The words are simple but profound: 'Jesus Christ, Son of the living God, have mercy on me, a sinner.' Or simply, 'Jesus'.

If you make this prayer while deepening your breathing you will almost certainly find that your mind turns more and more to Jesus and away from the concerns of the day.

Phrases from the Lord's Prayer can also be used in the same way. 'Abba, Father', for example, or 'Abba Father, glorify your name.'

Posture

Good posture can also help you relax and remain undistracted. The body should be relaxed but attentive. You should be comfortable but not strained or tense. Some people like to kneel. Others prefer to sit. Many like to use a prayer stool. Whichever way you choose, you will almost certainly find it helpful to keep your back straight and your head up – as though you were balancing a load.

Hands and arms can also express an openness to God which helps you concentrate on him. For example, the simple gesture of letting your hands lie in your lap with your palms turned upwards speaks of readiness to receive from God whatever he wants to give.

Visual Focus

Having a visual focus in your place of prayer can help to eliminate some distractions. When the eyes wander, the mind follows. If we keep our eyes open and gaze on a cross, a candle, a picture or another object our ability to concentrate on our prayer increases.

Epilogue

IT MATTERS HOW YOU LIVE

Prayer and life go together. They cannot be separated. We must be as firmly committed to live a peaceful life as to experience the peace of God in prayer. This is a pre-condition of contemplative prayer, as well as its fruit.

Among other things, this means that we must be whole-heartedly committed to follow the example of Jesus which we are shown in the Gospels – particularly in the Sermon on the Mount:

> no violence, no hatred no evil desire, no revenge, no judging, but gentleness, compassion, willingness to give and to share, an outgoing love and forgiveness for those who harm us.

We must endeavour to express our continued surrender by moving from violence to non-violent and peaceful ways,

- from any kind of falsehood to utter truthfulness and inner harmony,

- from self-assertion to greater sensitivity to the needs, rights and feelings of others,
- from self-indulgence to an instinct for purity of heart and mind,
- from possessiveness and greed to giving and sharing.

We must welcome with all our hearts the fruits of the Holy Spirit:

true love,
joy in the Spirit,
peace of heart,
patience,
kindness towards all,
goodness in our intentions,
trust in our dealings,
gentleness in inward and outward bearing
and self-control of heart and mind.

And all this becomes possible to the extent that we open our hearts and lives to the Spirit of Jesus. It also involves a continual return to repentance.

I have also found that it is necessary to keep the heart and mind free for contemplative prayer through a simple and sober life-style and through avoiding escapist habits such as compulsive reading of novels or watching too much TV. If we keep our hearts and minds free for God, we will occasionally enjoy his good gifts of reading and TV but true contemplative prayer is incompatible with the escapist habits which can overload our minds and bind our hearts.

Nourishing a Desire for God

We must also nourish within ourselves a constant desire for God. We may not have the same intensity of feeling but we may find ourselves identifying with the author of *The Cloud of Unknowing* who wrote the following about this attraction to God:

> If it happens that this attraction that you feel in reading or hearing about [contemplative love of God] is of itself so overwhelming that it goes to bed with you, gets up with you in the morning, accompanies you all day in all you do, separates you from normal daily exercises by inserting itself between your prayers and you; if it is associated with and follows your desire to the extent that it seems to be just the one desire, or you scarcely know what it is that alters your outlook and brings a cheerful smile to your lips; if, while it lasts, everything is a consolation and nothing can upset you; if you would run a thousand miles to have speech with someone whom you know has truly felt as you do; if, when you get there, you have nothing to say, no matter who speaks to you, since you do not wish to speak except about that one thing; if your words are few, but full of unction and fire; if one brief word of yours holds a world full of wisdom but seems mere foolishness to those who have not passed beyond reason; if your silence is peaceful, your speech edifying, your prayer secret, your pride proper, your behaviour modest, your laughter very soft; if your delight is that of a child at play; if you love to be alone and sit apart because you feel that others would hinder you, unless

> they did what you are doing; if you do not wish to read or listen to reading unless it be about this one thing; then indeed ...'[18]

there is evidence that you are drawn to true contemplative prayer which is beyond words and thoughts.

There are two ways of nourishing, feeding and strengthening this heart-longing for God. One way is to learn the art of *Lectio Divina.* This is a kind of meditative spiritual reading of texts which draws us to God and to prayer. We read the Bible slowly, one small section at a time, allowing words and phrases to fill our mind heart with love and desire for God. Such meditation leads to contemplation.

As we meditate on the Bible in this way, hidden and new shades of meaning seem to come to us effortlessly. Little by little, we realise that this enlightening is the gift of God's Spirit. He goes on to give us an even more precious gift: intimacy with the Father.

The other way to nourish our desire for God is to ask for the gift of prayer:

> 'Lord,
> teach me how to pray,
> how to know and love you in silent prayer;
> Lord,
> pour your Spirit into me in all his fullness;
> let me be possessed by him,
> so that you may reign in me
> and through me.

A Few Final Reflections

Contemplative prayer should not be started lightly.

Start only when you are ready, and then, never look back.

The Lord loves you and needs you.

He is waiting for an opportunity to enter your life.

Once you have begun praying you will never be the same.

God will make use of you.

It will be the greatest thing in your life.

May he be praised.

Alleluia!

A Prayer

Lord Jesus,
When you visit my heart,
it is bathed in the light of truth, the world
loses all its attraction
and an inner love is burning.
Those who have tasted you hunger for more,
those who have drunk are thirsty for more,
but only those who love you,
are able to long for you.
Jesus,
be my joy now as you will be my reward.
May your glory dwell in me,
for every and always. Amen.

NOTES

Foreword

1. John V. Taylor, *The Go-Between God.* SCM Press 1975, p. 169.

Coming to God

1. See the Appendix in *Listening to God* by Joyce Huggett for suggested music. In addition, the following music tapes have been produced primarily to bring people into stillness:

Open to God – Joyce Huggett, Hodder and Stoughton.
Reaching Out – Simeon Wood and John Gerighty, Eagle.

2. *The Cloud of Unknowing,* Ed. Clifton Wolters, Penguin Classics, 1961, p. 68 (Written by an unknown English author in c. 1350 and translated into modern English by Clifton Wolters).
3. Ibid., p. 68.
4. St John of the Cross, *Poems,* trans. Roy Campbell, Penguin 1960, p. 27.
5. *The Cloud of Unknowing,* Trans. Clifton Wolters, Penguin Classics, 1961, pp. 107-108.
6. Ibid., p. 68.
7. Ibid,. p. 101.
8. Ibid.
9. Dom Vitalis Lehodey, OCR, *The Ways of Mental Prayer,* Gill, Dublin 1960, pt II, Ch IX, para. 2.

10. *The Cloud of Unknowing,* op. cit. p. 36.
11. Ibid., p. 68.
12. St John of the Cross.
13. Matt. 7:7.
14. C.S. Lewis *The Last Battle.*
15. *The Cloud of Unknowing* op. cit. p. 125.
16. Ibid., p. 96.
17. Ibid., p. 94.
18. *A Letter of Private Devotion* by the author of *The Cloud of Unknowing,* London, Burns and Oates, pp. 67-68.

Bibliography

Ashwin, Angela, *Heaven in Ordinary*, Mayhew McCrimmon

Dodson, Peter, *Contemplating the Word*, SPCK

Foster, Richard, *Celebration of Discipline*, Hodder & Stoughton

Hebblethwaite, Margaret, *Finding God in All Things*, Fount

Huggett, Joyce, *Listening to God*, Hodder & Stoughton

Huggett, Joyce, *Open to God*, Hodder & Stoughton

Huggett, Joyce, *The Smile of Love*, Hodder & Stoughton

Huggett, Joyce, *God's Springtime*, BRF

Sr Margaret Magdalen, *Jesus, Man of Prayer*, Hodder & Stoughton

Merton, Thomas, *Contemplative Prayer*, DLT

Petit, Ian, OSB, *The God Who Speaks*, DLT

Brother Ramon, *A Hidden Fire*, Marshall Pickering

Runcorn, David, *Space for God*, DLT

Toon, Peter, *Meditating upon God's Word*, DLT

Wiederkehr, Macrina, OSB, *A Tree Full of Angels*, Harper & Row

Wallis, Paul, *Rough Ways in Prayer*, SPCK

Wolters, Clifton (Ed), *The Cloud of Unknowing*, Penguin

Teaching Tapes

Huggett, Joyce, *Teach me to Pray*, Eagle
Huggett, Joyce, *Teach us To Pray*, Hodder & Stoughton
Huggett, Joyce, *God's Springtime*, Eagle

Music Tapes

Huggett, Joyce, *Open to God*, Hodder & Stoughton
Simeon & John, *Reaching Out*, Eagle

Finding the Still Point

Gerald O'Mahony

Writing from his past experience of severe mood swings, the author provides a means to understand and govern the movements of moods and feelings so as to find the 'still' point – the place of perfect balance.

'Finding the Still Point' writes Gerald O'Mahony, 'aims to help the reader modify or alter behaviour patterns . . . It underpins common sense with the basic belief that we are God's children, and therefore not rubbish; we are God's children, and therefore not God.'

'Many of us have been taught to ignore our moods and to bash on regardless . . . this book clearly shows that to ignore our moods is to ignore the Holy Spirit at work within us and amongst us . . . Gerald O'Mahony . . . helps us to see that spirituality . . . is an activity in which we are all engaged, whether we like it or not, and which affects every aspect of our lives.' – *Gerald Hughes, SJ, from his foreword*

Eagle   ISBN 978 0 86347 634 1

Wild Spirit of the Living God

Prayer poems for the journey

Russ Parker

Lord God of the wild wind of heaven,
Send us your warm wind,
Your fresh wind,
Your mighty wind;
It's what we want for Jesus' sake.

This magnificent, moving collection of prayer poems will thrill, inspire, heal, encourage and renew.

Divided into seven sections, Russ Parker's poems and prayers will help you on your journey through the following themes: The Wild Spirit - Healings on the Journey - Easter Risings - Hunger - Pathways - Rites of Passage.

Russ Parker has exercised a wide-ranging ministry in both Baptist and Anglican churches. He has been co-tutor in Pastoral Counselling at St John's College, Nottingham, and has published numerous books, including *Healing Dreams, Free to Fail* and *Healing Death's Wounds.* He is Director of the Acorn Christian Healing Foundation in Bordon, Hampshire.

Eagle 978 086347 6334

Invitation to Solitude and Silence

Ruth Barton

An invitation . . .

Would you like to meet God deeply and fully?
Do you want to escape from the daily demands and noise of life?

Ruth Barton invites you to an adventure of spiritual transformation. In this book she describes how she discovered the real presence of God - the God who is present through the practice of solitude and silence. Follow her in these pages on an adventure that will lead you to freedom and authenticity, allowing you to become the person God created you to be.

In each chapter Ruth Barton combines teaching and reflection with carefully selected activities and disciplines that will help you as you start to practice solitude and silence. Elijah the prophet is the biblical guide for this gentle journey. And Ruth Barton shares her own experiences and perspectives on the ups and downs you might experience on the way, as you discover and apply the clearly explained classical spiritual disciplines. Your inner being will benefit greatly from the surprising insights and freedoms that flow refreshingly from this often over-looked disciplines, that lie surprisingly light.

'If you would like to know the 'rest appropriate for the people of God', then enter the practice of solitude and silence with Ruth Barton as you guide.'
– Dallas Willard

Ruth Barton is a spiritual director, teacher and retreat leader. She is a cofounder of The Transforming Center, a community of Christian men and women who shape and care for the souls of leaders.

Eagle ISBN 978 086347 5955

Life Journey

Mary Fleeson

From Holy Island, the home of the most famous of all Celtic illuminated manuscripts, The Lindisfarne Gospels, comes this beautiful, meditative work of art in the ages-old creative Celtic tradition.

You will be amazed at the intricacy of Mary's painstaking work, accomplished over a period of six years, and marvel at the various artistic threads and sources of inspiration. But, more importantly, you will be drawn into a deep stillness with God, a peace that becomes a Christ-centred life. And you will be challenged by the profundity of her poetry, and inspired by the way in which calligraphy and art combine to confront and challenge our perceptions and urge us into a deeper life with God.

'Mary Fleeson weaves her deeply creative talent as artist and poet, her intimate and profound knowledge of God, and her gentle but honest approach to life to make up this compelling call and journey into faith. I hope this unique book will lead or refresh many in their pilgrimage into prayer and journey into life.'
– Father Damian SSF, Vicar of Holy Island

'Mark came to Holy Island (Lindisfarne) to live God-centred lives within the small but challenging community there. Mary's creativity reflects all the creative strands imbued within the landscape and tradition of Holy Island, home to the Lindisfarne Gospels, in her vibrant organic images, her scribal work, and her words.' – Dr Michelle Brown, Curator of Illuminated Manuscripts, British Library

Eagle ISBN 978 086347 5160

One Man's Journey to Heaven

An illustrated life of Christ in calligraphy and tapestry

Sue Symons

'What is your first response to these images? Here at Bath Abbey our responses have often followed a similar pattern. First of all, there is the simple awed recognition, 'They're beautiful'. That instant impression then develops into an appreciation of the richness of the images and the presence of more than it is possible to absorb in one viewing. A common strategy, at this point, is to manage the multitude by focussing on a single dimension in each successive page, perhaps the decoration of the text or the symbolism of the textiles. Knowing that it isn't possible to take in everything at once viewers then find themselves drawn back to look again, to take in the texts, colours, textures, patterns, symbols, detailing and the music. Like the Jesus on whom these images meditate, these multi-dimensional diptychs respond to the viewer in a stream of generosity.'
– The Revd Dr Alan Garrow, Vicar Theologian, Bath Abbey

Inspired by *The Book of Kells* and other gloriously illuminated manuscripts, the intricate needlework tapestries and calligraphy in this book are the labour of love of artist Sue Symons. Sue interprets thirty five episodes from the life of Christ from the Annunciation to the Ascension, each with two images. The relevant Bible text as well as the artist's notes accompany each diptych.

Sue Symons is an accomplished artist in a number of media. She has exhibited in North America and the UK, and currently lives near Bath. All the images in this book form what are known as The Bath Abbey Diptychs, which as such are on view in a number of locations throughout the country.

Eagle 978 086347 6327